Cryptocurrency 101

Your Simple Path to Bitcoin Proficiency

Navigating the Digital Currency Landscape

DocThomaz

Potter's Wheel Publishing House
Minneapolis

Cryptocurrency 101: Your Simple Path to Bitcoin Proficiency is your essential guide through the cryptocurrency landscape. Authored by the experienced team at DocThomaz, this book simplifies complex concepts and provides comprehensive insights into the world of digital currencies. It's the perfect starting point for anyone eager to learn about the future of finance.

Disclaimer

This book is intended for educational purposes only and should not be considered as investment advice. The information provided is based on the authors' experiences and research and does not guarantee any specific financial outcome. Readers should exercise their own discretion and consult with professional financial advisors before making any investment decisions.

Cryptocurrency 101: Your Simple Path to Bitcoin Proficiency
Navigating the Digital Currency Landscape

Published by POTTER'S WHEEL PUBLISHING HOUSE
MINNEAPOLIS, MN 55378
www.POTTERSWHEELPUBLISHING.com

For permissions, contact:
info@POTTERSWHEELPUBLISHING.com

ISBN: 978-1-950399-20-8

To Everyone Who Dreams
and Strives for Financial
Independence.

Chapter Overview

Foreword

As we stand on the threshold of a new era in finance, *Cryptocurrency 101: Your Simple Path to Bitcoin Proficiency* emerges as a beacon for those navigating the often mystifying world of digital currencies. In this foreword, it is my privilege to introduce a book that not only demystifies the realm of cryptocurrency but does so with a clarity and insight that are rare in today's financial literature.

Cryptocurrency, once a fringe concept known only to tech enthusiasts and visionary investors, has rapidly transformed into a global phenomenon. Its ascent challenges not only our traditional understanding of money but also our beliefs in financial sovereignty and global connectivity. Amidst this backdrop, DocThomaz's work arrives as a much-needed guide for the curious, the cautious, and the ambitious.

What makes *Cryptocurrency 101: Your Simple Path to Bitcoin Proficiency* unique is not just its comprehensive exploration of digital currencies but its ability to make the complex seem approachable. This book is not an esoteric treatise filled with jargon but a clear, concise map that leads the reader through the twists and turns of blockchain technology, the mechanics of Bitcoin, and the nuances of wallet security, among other topics. It is as much for the beginner taking their first steps as it is for the seasoned investor seeking to broaden their understanding.

DocThomaz, through their collective expertise, weaves a narrative that is both educational and engaging. Their experience as investors and educators shines through each chapter, equipping readers with the knowledge and confidence to partake in the cryptocurrency revolution. They debunk myths, counter skepticism with facts, and present a balanced view of the risks and rewards that lie within the digital economy.

As we advance into an age where the lines between the physical and digital continue to blur, understanding cryptocurrency becomes not just an interest but a necessity. Whether you aim to invest, innovate, or simply be informed, this book is your starting point.

In reading *Cryptocurrency 101: Your Simple Path to Bitcoin Proficiency*, you embark on a journey of discovery. It's a journey that uncovers the potential of digital currencies to redefine our concepts of wealth, trade, and community. It's a journey that, much like the cryptocurrency landscape itself, is evolving and exhilarating.

Welcome to the world of Bitcoin and beyond. Welcome to *Cryptocurrency 101: Your Simple Path to Bitcoin Proficiency*.

Introduction

Unlocking the World of Cryptocurrency with DocThomaz

Dive into the transformative world of cryptocurrency with *Cryptocurrency 101: Your Simple Path to Bitcoin Proficiency* This book is your gateway to understanding the complexities of digital currencies and blockchain technology. Whether you're starting from scratch or looking to expand your knowledge, our guide is tailored to demystify the realm of digital finance.

Chapter 1

What Is Money, Anyway?

1.1 Money Through the Ages

Terminology:

Barter System: This is how people traded before money existed. They exchanged goods or services directly.

Explanation: Imagine a world without money, where you had to trade things directly. For instance, you might exchange a chicken for a bag of rice. This was the barter system, and it had its challenges. What if you had a chicken but needed a plow, and the plow owner didn't want a chicken? That's where money comes in.

1.2 The Birth of Money

Terminology:

Commodity Money: Money that has intrinsic value, like gold or silver.

Explanation: People realized that trading with goods had limitations, so they started using things like gold and silver as money. These were valuable by themselves and had a set worth, making trade easier. Think of gold coins from fairy tales – they're a form of commodity money.

1.3 Enter Traditional Currency

Terminology:

Fiat Money: Money that has value because the government says it does.

Explanation: Governments introduced paper money, which is what we use today. It doesn't have intrinsic value like gold, but the government says it's worth something. So, when you use a $10 bill, it's valuable because the government and people agree it is.

1.4 The Rise of Cryptocurrencies

Terminology:

Cryptocurrency: Digital or virtual money that uses cryptography for security.

Explanation: Cryptocurrencies are like digital coins, but they're stored on a computer. Bitcoin is a famous example. It's different from traditional money because it isn't physical – it's all online. It's like having money in a video game, but you can use it in the real world.

1.5 Comparing Money Types

Terminology:

Decentralized Monetary System: A system where no single entity, like a government or bank, controls something.

This utilizes cryptocurrencies via Blockchain technology which is like a digital ledger.

Explanation: Traditional money is controlled by governments and banks, but cryptocurrencies are decentralized. No one big authority tells them what they're worth. They also use blockchain technology, which is like a public record of all transactions. It's secure and transparent, so everyone can see it.

1.6 Cryptocurrencies Today

Terminology:

Bitcoin: The first and most well-known cryptocurrency.

Wallet: A digital place to store your cryptocurrencies.

Explanation: Today, cryptocurrencies are a hot topic. Bitcoin, for example, started as a digital experiment but is now worth a lot. People use digital wallets to store their cryptocurrencies, just like you use a physical wallet for cash.

1.7 Conclusion

In this chapter, we've traced the evolution of money from the barter system to the advent of digital currencies like Bitcoin. Highlighting the shift from physical commodity money and government-backed fiat to decentralized cryptocurrencies, the chapter emphasizes the revolutionary role of blockchain technology. This foundational chapter sets the stage for a deeper exploration of cryptocurrencies, their workings, and their growing significance in the financial world.

Chapter 2

A Brief History of Money

In this chapter, we'll embark on a journey through time to explore the fascinating evolution of money, beyond the days of barter to the rise of digital currencies like Bitcoin. Along the way, we'll encounter key terminologies, historical examples, and relatable comparisons to help you grasp the evolution of money.

1. Barter System: The Early Days

The barter system was like an ancient trading game, where people exchanged goods directly without using any standardized form of money. For instance, imagine trading your excess crop of apples for your neighbor's surplus of potatoes.

2. Commodity Money: A Step Forward

Commodity money was a clever invention. It's when items like gold, silver, or even salt became accepted as a medium of exchange because they had intrinsic value. Picture using shiny gold nuggets to buy goods, just like in pirate stories.

3. The Birth of Coins: A Standardized Form

Coins were a game-changer. They were bits of metal with a designated value, making trade easier. Think of them as the first official tokens, like modern-day quarters or dimes.

4. Paper Money: From Promissory Notes to Bills

Paper money started as promissory notes, essentially IOUs. Instead of carrying heavy bags of coins, people could use these notes as a promise that they could exchange for something valuable later. It's a bit like having a gift card you can use at a store.

5. Central Banking and Fiat Money

Fiat money is what we use today – currency without intrinsic value, but it's recognized by a government as legal tender. It's like monopoly money but with real purchasing power, thanks to a government's declaration.

6. Digital Currencies: The Bitcoin Revolution

Imagine digital currency as the money you can't touch. It's like transferring funds electronically. Bitcoin is a prime example – it's like having a special online coin that you can send or receive with a click, without a bank in between.

7. Comparing Ancient and Modern: From Shells to Cryptocurrencies

Cryptocurrencies like Bitcoin are like digital shells – they have value because people believe in them, just as ancient societies believed in shells as money. It's a leap from physical to digital, but the concept is somewhat similar.

8. The Future of Money: A Glimpse Ahead

We're moving towards a world where more people are using digital currencies in their daily lives. It's akin to seeing the transition from paper checks to credit cards – only this time, it's virtual wallets and cryptocurrencies taking the lead.

Through these historical examples and relatable comparisons, you'll gain a deeper understanding of how money has evolved over time, from barter to digital currencies. The next step is exploring the future of money and how it might continue to shape our financial landscapes.

Conclusion:

This chapter explores the historical evolution of money, tracing its journey beyond the ancient barter system to the innovative emergence of digital currencies like Bitcoin. It examines the transition from tangible commodity money, such as gold and silver, to the invention of coins and paper money, leading up to the modern concept of fiat money, which is backed by government decree. The narrative reaches a crescendo with the advent of digital currencies, emphasizing the significant shift from physical to digital assets and projecting a future marked by the widespread adoption of cryptocurrencies. This exploration provides a thorough understanding of the development of monetary systems and their ongoing impact on the financial landscape.

Chapter 3

The Birth of Bitcoin

In this chapter, we will dive into the fascinating story of Bitcoin's creation and the mysterious figure known as Satoshi Nakamoto. We'll unravel the mystery using easy-to-understand terms, historical examples, and relatable comparisons to shed light on how this revolutionary digital currency came to be.

1. The Digital Revolution: From Barter to Bitcoin

We'll start by briefly touching on how the concept of money evolved throughout history, from the days of barter to the digital age. Imagine trading your goods and services directly for what you need – like swapping your homemade cookies for a friend's hand-knit scarf. We'll explain how physical currency transformed into digital transactions, just as we now pay for things online without physical cash.

2. The Need for a New Currency: The Great Recession

We'll discuss the economic crisis of 2008 and its role in inspiring Bitcoin. Think of this like a modern-day example of a financial disaster, similar to the Great Depression but in recent times. The chaos led to a loss of trust in traditional banks and financial systems, which planted the seeds for an alternative.

3. Satoshi Nakamoto: The Wizard Behind the Curtain

Now, let's introduce the enigmatic figure, Satoshi Nakamoto. We'll compare this to famous masked figures in history, like the mysterious "Banksy" in the art world. Nakamoto is the pseudonymous creator of Bitcoin, and we'll explore the genius behind the concept.

4. The Whitepaper: Bitcoin's Blueprint

We'll explain how Nakamoto released a whitepaper, a bit like a recipe book, outlining how Bitcoin would work. We'll use the analogy of a secret formula revealed to the world, much like the recipe for Coca-Cola — known by only a few, but impacting many.

5. Mining for Gold: How Bitcoin Is Created

To make Bitcoin work, we'll discuss the role of miners. Think of miners like people digging for gold in a digital world. We'll explain how they solve complex math problems to validate transactions and create new Bitcoins.

6. The Halving: Digital Scarcity in the 21st Century

Imagine if gold mines produced less gold over time — this is similar to what happens in the Bitcoin world through an event called "the halving." We'll unravel the concept of how the reward for miners is reduced, making Bitcoin scarcer and more valuable.

7. Bitcoin's Impact Today: The Modern Gold Rush

We'll wrap up the chapter by comparing Bitcoin to a modern-day gold rush. People and companies are investing in Bitcoin, much like prospectors did during historical gold rushes. We'll also touch on its impact on the financial industry and the ongoing quest to uncover the identity of Satoshi Nakamoto.

By using these relatable examples and straightforward explanations, readers will gain a deeper understanding of how Bitcoin came into existence and why it continues to capture the world's imagination.

Chapter 4

How Bitcoin Works

In this chapter, we'll dive into the technical aspects of Bitcoin, breaking it down into digestible pieces so that even beginners can grasp the concept. We'll use simple terms, historical examples, and comparisons to make it relatable and easy to understand.

1. What is Bitcoin?

Explanation: Bitcoin is a digital currency that exists only in the digital world. It's like regular money but purely digital, meaning you can't hold a physical Bitcoin coin. Instead, it's stored in a digital wallet on your computer or smartphone.

Relatable Example: Think of it as the evolution of money. We started with physical coins and bills, then credit cards, and now we have digital currency like Bitcoin.

2. Blockchain Technology

Explanation: Bitcoin uses a technology called blockchain to keep track of transactions. A blockchain is like a digital ledger that records all Bitcoin transactions. It's stored on a network of computers, making it very secure and transparent.

Relatable Example: Imagine it as a public ledger in a library where every transaction is written down for everyone to see, and no one can tamper with it.

3. Decentralization

Explanation: Bitcoin is decentralized, meaning there's no central authority like a government or bank controlling it. Instead, a network of computers (called nodes) maintains the system.

Relatable Example: It's like a community garden where everyone contributes, and no single person owns it. This ensures fairness and prevents one person from making all the rules.

4. Wallets and Private Keys

Explanation: Your Bitcoin is stored in a digital wallet, which is like a digital bank account. You access it with a private key, which is like your secret password.

Relatable Example: Think of your wallet as your bank account, and the private key as your ATM pin. Only you should know your pin to access your funds.

5. Mining

Explanation: Mining is the process of confirming and adding transactions to the blockchain. Miners use powerful computers to solve complex math problems, and in return, they're rewarded with new Bitcoins.

Relatable Example: It's like a digital gold rush where people use their computers to dig for new Bitcoins. The first one to solve the puzzle gets the reward.

6. Transactions

Explanation: When you send Bitcoin to someone, you create a digital transaction. This transaction is added to the blockchain, making it transparent and irreversible.

Relatable Example: It's similar to sending an email. Once you hit "send," you can't take it back; it's out there for the recipient to see.

7. Security

Explanation: Bitcoin is secure because of complex cryptography. Your private key ensures that only you can access your Bitcoins. Plus, the blockchain's decentralized nature makes it resistant to tampering.

Relatable Example: Comparison: It's like having an unbreakable digital lock on your wallet, and many people are guarding it, making it extremely secure.

8. Bitcoin vs Altcoins

Bitcoin:

Strengths: Bitcoin, being the first cryptocurrency, has the most recognition and widespread adoption. It's often viewed as a "digital gold," serving as a store of value and a hedge against inflation. Its network is highly secure, with a proven track record.

Weaknesses: Bitcoin faces issues with scalability and slower transaction speeds compared to some altcoins. Its technology is also not as versatile for developing decentralized applications.

Altcoins:

Strengths: Many altcoins offer enhanced functionality, such as faster transaction speeds, lower fees, and more flexible and advanced technological capabilities (like smart contracts in Ethereum). They often address specific niches and use cases.

Weaknesses: Altcoins generally have lower market capitalization and can be more volatile, often featuring less security and recognition compared to Bitcoin. They may also face a higher risk of failure. However, those within the top 100 by market capitalization are usually more stable and considered safer investments compared to lesser-known altcoins.

Investment Implications: Bitcoin is often considered a safer, more stable investment in the crypto world, but with potentially lower returns compared to some high-growth altcoins. Altcoins can offer higher returns but come with increased risk. Diversification across different cryptocurrencies can be a strategy to balance these risks and rewards.

9. Bitcoin Cycle

The Bitcoin cycle refers to the recurring patterns of market behavior, typically characterized by periods of rapid price increase (bull markets) and periods of decline (bear markets).

Bull Markets: These phases are marked by increasing investor optimism, rising prices, and higher trading volumes. They can be driven by factors like technological advancements, positive regulatory developments, or broader economic factors.

Bear Markets: These periods are characterized by pessimism, declining prices, and often lower trading volumes. They can be triggered by regulatory crackdowns, technological issues, or shifts in investor sentiment.

These cycles can be illustrated through a Bitcoin price chart, showing the historical pattern of peaks (highs of bull markets) and troughs (lows of bear markets).

10. Bitcoin Halvening

The Bitcoin halving (or halvening) is a scheduled event that occurs approximately every four years, where the reward for mining Bitcoin transactions is halved. This process is a part of Bitcoin's deflationary monetary policy designed to mimic the extraction of a finite resource, similar to gold mining.

Impact on Supply: Each halving reduces the rate at which new bitcoins are created, thus slowing down the supply growth. This decreased supply growth can create upward pressure on the price, assuming steady or increasing demand.

Impact on Price: Historically, halving events have preceded some of the most significant bull runs in Bitcoin's price. However, it's important to note that past performance doesn't guarantee future results, and numerous other factors also influence Bitcoin's price.

A chart depicting Bitcoin's price over time, with markers indicating the halving events, can visually illustrate the historical impact of these events on Bitcoin's price. However, it's essential to consider the broader market context when interpreting these trends.

11. Bitcoin Today vs. the Past

Explanation: In the early days, Bitcoin was worth very little, and few people used it. But today, it's a recognized digital asset, and you can use it for various things, from buying goods to investing.

Relatable Example: Think of it like a small, unknown company growing into a big, well-known corporation. Bitcoin started as an experiment but now has real value in the world.

By understanding these fundamental aspects of how Bitcoin works, you'll be better equipped to appreciate its significance and navigate the world of cryptocurrency with confidence.

Chapter 5

The Blockchain Revolution

In this chapter, we'll explore the fascinating world of blockchain technology and its revolutionary impact. We'll break down the concepts and potential influence of blockchain with simple terminologies and relatable examples.

1. The Birth of Bitcoin

In 2009, an anonymous person named Satoshi Nakamoto created Bitcoin, the first cryptocurrency that relies on blockchain technology. It was like the birth of digital gold, a new way of money without banks.

2. How Does Blockchain Work?

Terminology:

Decentralized: This means there's no central authority (like a bank) controlling the blockchain. It's like a democracy for data.

Explanation: In a traditional system, banks keep a record of all your transactions, and you have to trust them. With blockchain, everyone has a copy of the record, and they all check and verify it. No single person or entity has all the power, making it fair and secure.

3. Real-World Applications

Relatable Examples:

- **Supply Chain Management:** Companies use blockchain to track the journey of products from the factory to your hands.

For instance, you can trace your coffee back to the exact farm it came from.

- **Voting Systems:** Some countries are exploring blockchain for elections, ensuring transparency and preventing fraud.
- **Smart Contracts:** These are like digital agreements that execute themselves when conditions are met. For example, you could use a smart contract to automatically release payment once a product is delivered.

4. Challenges and the Future

Terminology:

Scalability: This is about making blockchain work faster and handle more transactions, just like upgrading a road to handle more traffic.

Explanation: Right now, blockchain can be slow and use lots of energy. Imagine if your favorite game took hours to load. But developers are working on improving it, so it can be used for everything from daily transactions to streaming video.

5. The Impact on Our Lives

Comparing Past and Present:

Just as the internet changed how we communicate, blockchain has the potential to transform how we trust, exchange, and record things. It's like moving from sending letters to sending emails — faster, cheaper, and more open.

Terminology:

Financial Inclusion: Using blockchain to give access to banking services to people who don't have traditional banks, like in remote villages.

Explanation: Think of it as giving everyone in the world a virtual bank account, making it easier for them to save, spend, and invest, even if they don't live near a physical bank.

As we dive deeper into this chapter, you'll discover the blockchain revolution's potential to change the way we do business, manage our data, and even vote. It's a technology that has the power to bring more fairness, security, and opportunities into our lives.

Chapter 6

Owning and Storing Bitcoin: A Practical Guide

In this chapter, we'll delve into the essential aspects of purchasing, possessing, and safely storing your digital assets, particularly Bitcoin. We'll make sure to use plain language and relatable examples to help you navigate the world of cryptocurrencies.

1. Acquiring Bitcoin:

Exchange: Think of a cryptocurrency exchange as a digital marketplace where you can buy, sell, and trade Bitcoin. It's like a modern version of a stock exchange, but for digital currencies. One popular exchange, Coinbase, is like a cryptocurrency bank where you can create an account and purchase Bitcoin just as you would with traditional money.

Wallet: A Bitcoin wallet is like your personal digital piggy bank. It's where you keep your Bitcoin. There are different types of wallets, such as online wallets (similar to your email account) and hardware wallets (like a secure USB drive). Historical lesson: Mt. Gox was an early exchange where people stored their Bitcoin, but it got hacked in 2014, resulting in a major loss of Bitcoin for users.

2. Bitcoin vs Altcoins: Understanding the Differences and Investment Implications

Explanation:

Bitcoin, the first cryptocurrency, differs significantly from altcoins (alternative coins).

Bitcoin: Known for its pioneering status and widespread recognition, Bitcoin is often seen as a digital gold, offering a store of value and a hedge against inflation. Its primary strengths include its established network, widespread adoption, and perceived security. However, Bitcoin also has limitations, like slower transaction speeds and higher transaction costs compared to some altcoins.

Altcoins: These encompass a wide range of cryptocurrencies that emerged after Bitcoin. Altcoins, such as Ethereum, Solana, Ripple (XRP), and Litecoin, often aim to address the perceived shortcomings of Bitcoin by offering faster transactions, lower fees, or additional functionalities like smart contracts (Ethereum). Altcoins can offer innovative use cases but often come with increased risks, including lower market capitalization, less liquidity, and a higher likelihood of volatility.

Investment Implications:

Diversification: Investors often diversify their portfolio with a mix of Bitcoin and altcoins to balance risk and potential rewards.

Risk Assessment: Bitcoin is generally considered less risky compared to altcoins due to its established market presence. Altcoins, while potentially offering higher returns, often come with a higher risk profile.

3. Blue-chip Crypto Coins: Defining and Identifying Top-Tier Cryptocurrencies

Explanation:

Blue-chip cryptocurrencies are the ones considered to be the most stable, reliable, and less volatile in the crypto market. These are typically the coins with the largest market capitalizations, strong use-cases, high liquidity, and widespread adoption. They are akin to blue-chip stocks in the stock market, representing well-established companies.

Characteristics: A blue-chip crypto coin typically has a proven track record of stability, robust technological foundation, strong community and developer support, and a significant degree of adoption in the cryptocurrency ecosystem.

Examples:

- **Bitcoin (BTC):** Often considered the primary blue-chip cryptocurrency, given its status as the first and most well-known digital currency.
- **Ethereum (ETH):** Known for its smart contract functionality and as a platform for decentralized applications (dApps).
- **Binance Coin (BNB):** Originally a utility token for the Binance cryptocurrency exchange, it has grown in use and stability.
- **Ripple (XRP):** Aims to facilitate faster, more affordable cross-border transactions, and is widely used by various financial institutions.

Investment Implications:

- **Stability and Growth:** Investors often view blue-chip cryptocurrencies as more stable investment options in the volatile crypto market. They tend to show consistent growth and resilience during market downturns.

- **Long-term Investment:** Due to their stability, blue-chip cryptos are frequently chosen for long-term investment strategies.

Both Bitcoin and blue-chip cryptocurrencies play distinct roles in an investor's portfolio, offering a balance between stability, risk, and potential returns. Understanding their differences and implications is crucial for informed investment decisions.

4. Owning Bitcoin:

- **Public and Private Keys:** These are like your Bitcoin's address and secret code. The public key is your address that you give to people when they want to send you Bitcoin. The private key is your secret password that you must keep safe. Imagine your public key is your home's address, and your private key is the key to your front door. If someone else gets your private key, they can access your Bitcoin. Historical example: In 2013, James Howells accidentally threw away a hard drive with his private keys, containing Bitcoin worth millions, in a landfill.

5. Safely Storing Bitcoin:

- **Cold Storage:** This is like putting your savings in a safety deposit box at a bank. Cold storage means keeping your Bitcoin offline, away from the internet, making it less susceptible to hacking. An example is a hardware wallet, which is a bit like a USB stick that holds your Bitcoin securely. Historical example: In 2010, a programmer named Laszlo Hanyecz made the first-known real-world purchase using Bitcoin when he bought two pizzas for 10,000 Bitcoins. If he'd securely stored those Bitcoins, they'd be worth a fortune today.

- **Two-Factor Authentication (2FA):** 2FA is an extra layer of security, like using both a key and a PIN to access your bank account. When you enable 2FA for your Bitcoin wallet or exchange account, it adds another barrier for anyone trying to access your assets.

- **Backup Your Wallet:** Backing up your wallet is like making a copy of your important documents. If you lose your wallet or it gets damaged, having a backup ensures you won't lose your Bitcoin.

By understanding these key concepts and learning from past examples, you can make informed decisions about acquiring, owning, and securing your Bitcoin, ensuring you have a safe and prosperous journey in the world of digital assets.

Chapter 7

Altcoins and the Cryptocurrency Ecosystem

In this Chapter we dive into the fascinating world of alternative cryptocurrencies, often referred to as "altcoins," and explore the broader cryptocurrency market. This chapter is designed to provide you with a comprehensive understanding of altcoins, their significance, and their role in the evolving crypto landscape.

1. What Are Altcoins?

Terminology: Altcoins (Alternative Coins)

Explanation: Altcoins are any cryptocurrencies other than Bitcoin. They are the alternative players in the cryptocurrency market.

Relatable Example: Litecoin (LTC) was one of the earliest altcoins, created in 2011. It offered faster transaction confirmation times compared to Bitcoin. Another recent example is Solana (SOL).

2. Why Altcoins?

Explanation: Altcoins were created to address limitations or offer variations compared to Bitcoin. For example, some aim to improve transaction speed, privacy, or smart contract functionality.

Relatable Example: Ethereum (ETH) introduced the concept of smart contracts, allowing developers to build decentralized applications on its blockchain.

3. Types of Altcoins

Terminology: Forks, Tokens

Explanation: Altcoins can be created in two main ways. Forks are when a new cryptocurrency is created by modifying the code of an existing one. Tokens are built on existing blockchain platforms and represent assets or utility.

Relatable Example: Bitcoin Cash (BCH) is a fork of Bitcoin, while Chainlink (LINK) is an example of a token built on the Ethereum blockchain.

4. The Role of Altcoins

Explanation: Altcoins serve various purposes. Some aim to be digital cash (like Bitcoin), while others focus on privacy (Monero/XMR), governance (Tezos/XTZ), or stable value (Tether/USDT).

Relatable Example: Ripple (XRP) was created to facilitate faster and cheaper cross-border payments for banks and financial institutions.

5. Altcoins and Innovation

Terminology: Decentralized Finance (DeFi), Non-Fungible Tokens (NFTs)

Explanation: Altcoins have driven innovation. DeFi protocols enable lending, borrowing, and trading without traditional intermediaries. NFTs represent ownership of unique digital assets.

Relatable Example: DeFi projects like Aave (AAVE) have created lending platforms, and NFTs have gained popularity through projects like CryptoKitties.

6. The Risks and Rewards of Altcoins

Explanation: Altcoins can offer high returns but come with higher risk due to their volatility. Research is essential before investing in them.

Relatable Example: Many altcoins experienced significant price increases during the 2017 bull run, but some later saw substantial losses.

7. Altcoins Today

Explanation: The crypto ecosystem has evolved, with thousands of altcoins available. Some have gained prominence, while others have faded into obscurity.

Relatable Example: Dogecoin (DOGE), initially created as a meme, gained significant attention in 2021, partly due to endorsements by notable figures like Elon Musk.

8. Altcoins and Portfolio Diversification

Explanation: Including a variety of altcoins in your investment portfolio can spread risk and capture diverse opportunities in the crypto market.

Historical Example: Bitcoin's dominance in the market has decreased as more altcoins have gained popularity, showing the appeal of diversification.

9. Top Crypto Categories/Types Based on CoinGecko

Utility Tokens:

Explanation: Utility tokens are digital assets designed for specific uses within a blockchain ecosystem. They grant users access to products or services and can be used for transactions within a particular project. For example, Binance Coin (BNB) is used to pay for transaction fees on the Binance exchange and participate in token sales.

Security Tokens:

Explanation: Security tokens represent investment contracts into an underlying investment asset, like stocks, bonds, or real estate. They often provide rights such as ownership, dividend distribution, and voting. Polymath (POLY) is an example, enabling users to create and manage security tokens on the blockchain.

Stablecoins:

Explanation: Stablecoins are cryptocurrencies designed to minimize the volatility typically associated with cryptocurrencies. They are pegged to a stable asset like the US dollar. Tether (USDT) and USD Coin (USDC) are common examples, each theoretically backed one-to-one by US dollars.

Governance Tokens:

Explanation: Governance tokens allow holders to participate in decision-making processes of a decentralized project. Holding these tokens often grants voting rights on proposals that influence the direction and updates of the project. Maker (MKR) is an example, where holders can vote on changes to the MakerDAO ecosystem.

DeFi Tokens:

Explanation: DeFi tokens are associated with decentralized finance projects. These tokens often facilitate services like lending, borrowing, or yield farming in a decentralized manner. Aave (AAVE) is an example, where token holders can lend or borrow different cryptocurrencies and participate in the platform's governance.

Meme Coins:

Explanation: Meme coins are cryptocurrencies that originated from internet jokes or memes. Unlike other cryptocurrencies, they often don't have a clear use case or fundamental value and are known for their volatility. Their value is heavily influenced by social media hype and community sentiment.

Examples and Risks: The most notable example is Dogecoin (DOGE), which started as a joke but gained significant popularity and value. Another example is Shiba Inu (SHIB), which also garnered attention due to its meme status. The risks associated with meme coins include their high volatility and susceptibility to market hype and speculation, making them risky investments. The price can be significantly influenced by endorsements from celebrities or social media influencers, leading to rapid price changes.

10. Tokenomics and Price: Understanding the Impact of Key Factors

Tokenomics, the study of the economic system within cryptocurrencies, plays a crucial role in shaping the price and value of digital tokens. Several factors, including all-time high, market cap, max supply, inflation, circulating supply, and max supply, significantly influence this dynamic landscape. Let's delve into each of these factors with explanations and examples for a clearer understanding.

All-Time High (ATH)

The Peak of a Cryptocurrency's Value

Explanation: The All-Time High (ATH) refers to the highest price point a cryptocurrency has ever reached in its trading history. It is often a psychological barrier, impacting investor sentiment and future price movements.

Example: If Bitcoin once reached $60,000, that would be its ATH. This figure becomes a benchmark for investors, indicating the potential peak value of the asset and often influencing future investment decisions.

Market Capitalization (Market Cap)

The Total Value of a Cryptocurrency in Circulation

Explanation: Market cap is calculated by multiplying the current price of a cryptocurrency by its total circulating supply. It provides a snapshot of the cryptocurrency's relative size and market dominance.

Example: If Ethereum has 115 million coins in circulation and each coin is worth $2,000, its market cap would be $230 billion. This metric helps investors understand Ethereum's market share and compare it to other cryptocurrencies.

Max Supply

The Ultimate Limit of Tokens

Explanation: Max supply is the maximum number of tokens that will ever exist for a cryptocurrency. It's a critical factor that influences the potential scarcity and long-term value of the token.

Example: Bitcoin has a max supply of 21 million coins. This limited supply creates scarcity, potentially increasing Bitcoin's value as the supply nears its maximum limit.

Inflation

The Rate at Which New Tokens Are Introduced

Explanation: Inflation in the context of cryptocurrencies refers to the rate at which new tokens are created and added to the total supply. High inflation can dilute the value of existing tokens, while low inflation rates can increase scarcity and potentially drive up value.

Example: A cryptocurrency with a high inflation rate might see its value decrease as the market is flooded with new tokens, reducing the rarity and value of each individual token.

Circulating Supply

The Number of Tokens Currently Available

Explanation: Circulating supply is the number of tokens that are currently available in the market and can be traded. It's different from the max supply, which is the total number that will ever exist.

Example: If there are 18 million Bitcoins in circulation out of a max supply of 21 million, the circulating supply is 18 million. This figure is crucial for calculating the market cap and understanding the current availability and liquidity of the cryptocurrency.

Tokenomics and Its Impact on Price

Combining Factors for a Holistic View

Explanation: The combination of these factors gives investors a comprehensive view of a cryptocurrency's economic model – its tokenomics. Understanding how ATH, market cap, max supply, inflation, and circulating supply interact helps investors make informed decisions. These elements collectively influence the supply-demand dynamics, perceived value, and long-term viability of a cryptocurrency.

Example: A cryptocurrency with a high market cap, low inflation, and a significant portion of its max supply already in circulation might be seen as a stable and potentially valuable investment. Conversely, a high inflation rate and a low percentage of max supply circulated can signal potential devaluation risks.

11. Phases of The Bitcoin Halving

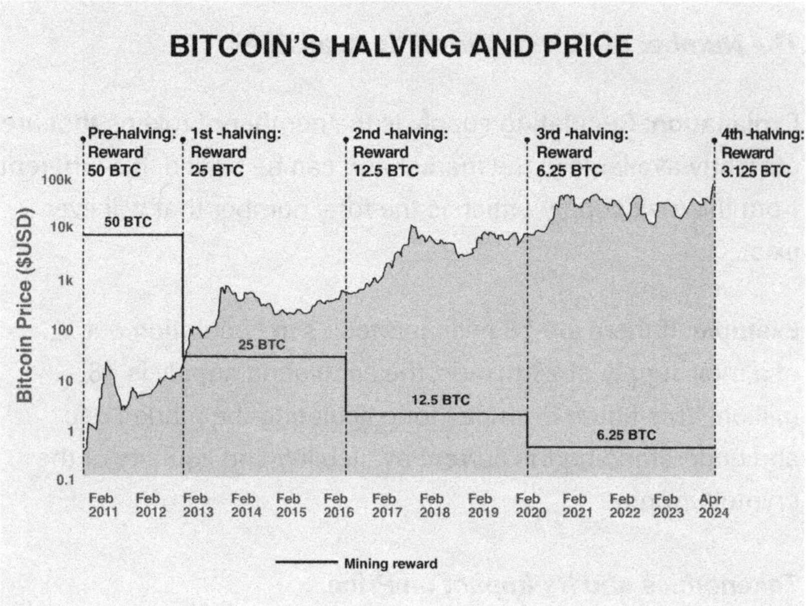

In simple terms, the Bitcoin halving is a big event that happens every few years where the reward for mining Bitcoin is cut in half. This can affect how much Bitcoin is worth and gets a lot of attention from people who invest in or use Bitcoin.

a. Getting Ready for the Halving

The Excitement Before the Change

Explanation: Think of the time before the Bitcoin halving like the buzz before a big holiday sale. People start talking and getting excited about what might happen. In the Bitcoin world, this means investors and traders are guessing how the halving will affect Bitcoin's price. For example, if a big sale is expected to cut prices in half, people start planning and talking about it weeks in advance. Similarly, before the 2020 Bitcoin halving, there was a lot of chatter and the price began to rise as people got ready for the big event. We're expecting another halving in 2024, where the reward will be reduced again, this time to 3.125 Bitcoins from 6.25 Bitcoins.

b. The Day of the Halving

Cutting the Bitcoin Rewards

Explanation: The halving is like a store suddenly giving out half as many rewards points for the same purchase. Before the halving, miners earn a certain number of Bitcoins for verifying transactions. The halving cuts this reward in half. So, if miners were getting 10 Bitcoins before, now they only get 5. This is a big deal because it means fewer new Bitcoins are coming into the market, which could make each Bitcoin more valuable.

c. Right After the Halving

The Market's Immediate Reaction

Explanation: Imagine everyone's reaction the day after a big policy change. Some are happy, some are not, and there's a lot of adjusting to do. Similarly, right after the Bitcoin halving, the market can be a bit shaky. Miners might be upset about getting fewer Bitcoins, and everyone's watching to see what happens to the price. It's like when a new rule is introduced in a game, and players are trying to figure out their next move.

d. Long-Term Effects

Seeing the Big Picture

Explanation: This is like watching a plant grow after you've changed how you water it. It doesn't grow overnight, but over weeks and months, you might see a big difference. After the Bitcoin halving, the price doesn't skyrocket immediately. But over time, as people realize there aren't as many new Bitcoins being made, the ones that are already out there can become more valuable. Think of it as a rare toy becoming more valuable because the company stopped making more of them.

e. Gearing Up for the Next Halving

Looking Ahead

Explanation: After the dust settles, it's like the end of the holiday season when stores start planning for next year's sale. In the Bitcoin world, people start thinking about how the next halving, which is a few years away, might affect things. They use what they learned from the last halving to guess what might happen next time. It's a cycle of anticipation, reaction, and reflection, always looking forward to the next big change.

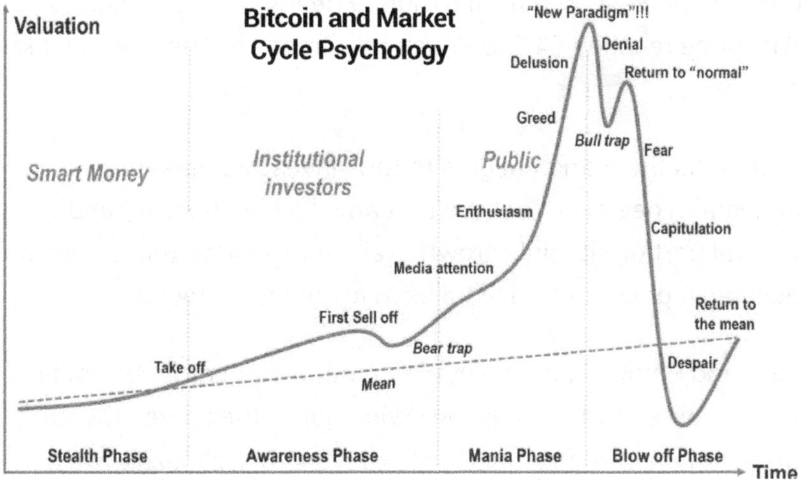

12. Understanding the Emotional Journey of Investors

Explanation: Bitcoin's market cycle is not just a reflection of economic factors; it's also a vivid display of collective investor psychology. This cycle typically moves through phases of optimism, euphoria, denial, fear, and eventually, hope and recovery.

Optimism and Belief: As Bitcoin's price begins to rise, there's a growing sense of optimism among investors. This phase is characterized by a belief in the long-term potential of Bitcoin. For example, when Bitcoin started recovering from a low point, investors started to believe in the future growth of the asset, leading to increased buying.

Euphoria: This is the peak of the cycle, where prices skyrocket, and irrational exuberance takes over. Investors may believe that the sky's the limit for Bitcoin prices. During the 2017 Bitcoin rally, the price soared from $1000 to nearly $20,000, and in 2021 BTC price reached 64,000 driven by a frenzy of speculation and euphoria.

Denial: As the market begins to turn, investors initially live in denial. They might believe that any dip is temporary and a natural part of Bitcoin's growth trajectory. During this phase, the decline in price is often dismissed as just a 'correction.'

Fear and Panic: When the market continues to drop, fear sets in. Investors start to panic, worrying about their investments plummeting in value. The rapid sell-off in March 2020, when Bitcoin prices dropped by about 50% in two days, is a classic example of this phase.

Despondency and Capitulation: This phase marks the bottom of the market cycle. Investors are despondent, often leading to a mass sell-off — a capitulation where they give up on their investments. It's the point where the market sentiment is at its lowest.

Hope and Recovery: Finally, the cycle moves into a phase of hope and gradual recovery. Those who held onto their investments start to see light at the end of the tunnel, and new investors are attracted by the lower prices, starting the cycle anew.

The psychology of the Bitcoin market cycle is critical because it drives the behaviors of investors, often leading to a self-fulfilling prophecy. Recognizing these emotional stages can help investors make more rational decisions, avoiding the pitfalls of getting swept up in market euphoria or panic.

13. The Interplay Between Bitcoin and Altcoin Market Cycles

The cryptocurrency market is known for its dynamic interplay between Bitcoin and altcoins (alternative coins to Bitcoin). Typically, this relationship follows a pattern where Bitcoin's price movements significantly influence the altcoin market. Here's a breakdown of how this cycle often unfolds:

Bitcoin Leads the Rally: The cycle usually starts with Bitcoin's price rising significantly. Bitcoin, being the most prominent and widely recognized cryptocurrency, often acts as a barometer for the entire crypto market. Investors tend to initially focus on Bitcoin due to its higher liquidity and established reputation.

Stabilization and Shift to Altcoins: After a substantial rally, when Bitcoin's price begins to stabilize or enter a consolidation phase, investors' attention shifts towards altcoins. This shift is partly driven by the perception that Bitcoin is 'overvalued' and the search for higher returns in the more volatile altcoin market.

Altcoin Season (Alt Season): This phase is characterized by the rapid price increase of altcoins. Altcoins often take turns surging in value, sometimes experiencing significant gains. This phenomenon, known as "Alt Season," can see many altcoins outperform Bitcoin in terms of percentage gains.

Correlation in Downtrends: However, the market also exhibits a high correlation during downturns. When Bitcoin experiences a significant drop in value, it often leads to a broader market sell-off, affecting altcoins as well. This reaction is typically more pronounced in altcoins, which can experience steeper declines compared to Bitcoin.

Magnitude of Movements: The volatility in altcoins is generally higher than in Bitcoin. This means that both the upswings and downswings can be more extreme. During a bullish phase, some altcoins can see astronomical rises, and conversely, during a bearish phase, they can face severe devaluations.

Example:

- **Bull Phase:** Bitcoin starts a bull run and reaches new all-time highs. After some time, its growth slows down or plateaus. Investors then divert their funds to altcoins like Ethereum, Ripple, or Litecoin, leading to a significant increase in these altcoins' prices.

- **Bear Phase:** When Bitcoin starts to fall, perhaps due to market saturation, regulatory news, or a global economic event, it triggers a market-wide sell-off. Altcoins, being more volatile, often experience a sharper decline, amplifying the market downturn.

Understanding the relationship between Bitcoin and altcoin cycles is crucial for investors to navigate the crypto market effectively. This pattern reflects the market's sentiment and risk appetite, where Bitcoin often acts as the initial driver of growth, followed by a speculative surge in altcoins, and eventually a correlated downturn.

This chapter delves into the world of alternative cryptocurrencies, known as altcoins, which offer diverse functionalities and innovations beyond Bitcoin. The chapter covers the reasons behind the creation of altcoins, like improved transaction speeds or enhanced privacy, and explains different types such as forks and tokens, using examples like Litecoin and Ethereum. It discusses the various roles altcoins play in the digital currency ecosystem, from being digital cash to facilitating cross-border payments, and introduces concepts like Decentralized Finance (DeFi) and Non-Fungible Tokens (NFTs). The chapter also highlights the risks and rewards associated with investing in altcoins and the importance of diversification in a crypto portfolio. Additionally, it delves into tokenomics, explaining factors like market cap and circulating supply, and examines the dynamics of Bitcoin and altcoin market cycles, emphasizing the interconnected nature of their price movements.

Chapter 8

Crypto in the Real World: From Everyday Transactions to Global Remittances

In this chapter, we'll explore how cryptocurrencies have made their way into our everyday lives, revolutionizing the way we handle transactions and global remittances. We'll break down some key terminologies and provide real-world examples to make this fascinating topic accessible to all.

1. Cryptocurrency Basics for Everyday Life

Terminology:

Cryptocurrency: Digital or virtual currencies that use cryptography for security.

Wallet: A digital tool for storing and managing your cryptocurrencies.

Blockchain: A decentralized and immutable ledger that records all cryptocurrency transactions.

Explanation: Cryptocurrencies, like Bitcoin and Ethereum, are digital currencies you can use for various transactions. To manage them, you need a "wallet," which is like a digital bank account. Every transaction is recorded on a "blockchain," which is a secure and transparent ledger.

Relatable Example: Buying Your Morning Coffee with Crypto

Terminology:

Merchant: A business that accepts cryptocurrency as a form of payment.

Transaction Confirmation: The process of verifying a crypto payment.

Digital Payment Gateway: An online service that facilitates cryptocurrency transactions.

Explanation: Imagine walking into your favorite coffee shop and using your cryptocurrency wallet to pay for that morning latte. Merchants worldwide are now accepting cryptocurrencies. The transaction is confirmed on the blockchain, ensuring secure and speedy payments, often with the help of digital payment gateways.

2. Remittances Made Easy

Terminology:

Remittance: Money sent from one location to another, often across borders.

Cross-Border Transaction: Financial transactions that involve two different countries.

Explanation: In the past, sending money to family or friends in another country could be expensive and slow. Cryptocurrencies have changed the game. Now, you can send money (remittances) quickly and with lower fees. This helps people support their loved ones across borders more efficiently.

3. The Evolution of Cryptocurrency

Terminology:

Bitcoin Pizza Day: An event in 2010 when the first real-world Bitcoin transaction occurred – two pizzas were bought for 10,000 BTC.

Altcoins: Any cryptocurrency other than Bitcoin.

NFTs (Non-Fungible Tokens): Digital assets representing ownership of unique items or content.

Explanation: Let's travel back to 2010 when someone spent 10,000 Bitcoins on two pizzas. Today, that would be worth millions! Since then, thousands of altcoins have emerged, each with its unique use cases. And, don't forget NFTs – they're like owning digital art or collectibles, showing the endless possibilities of blockchain technology.

4. Challenges and the Road Ahead

Terminology:

Volatility: Rapid and unpredictable price changes.

Regulation: Government rules and policies around cryptocurrencies.

Explanation: Cryptocurrencies can be incredibly volatile. Their prices can skyrocket or plummet in a matter of hours.

Additionally, governments are still figuring out how to regulate this new form of money. The road ahead for cryptocurrencies includes addressing these challenges to ensure a stable and secure financial landscape.

5. Cryptocurrency Exchange-Traded Funds

Cryptocurrency Exchange-Traded Funds (ETFs) are investment vehicles that track the performance of cryptocurrencies or a basket of different digital assets. Similar to traditional ETFs in the stock market, crypto ETFs allow investors to buy shares that represent underlying crypto assets. These ETFs trade on regular stock exchanges, making them accessible to a wider range of investors who might not be comfortable or equipped to deal with the direct purchase and storage of cryptocurrencies.

6. Government Policy: The Impact of Regulations on Cryptocurrency

Explanation:

Government policies wield a powerful influence on the cryptocurrency market, shaping its trajectory and dynamics. These policies range from supportive measures, such as providing clear tax guidelines and legal status for digital assets, to more restrictive actions like outright bans or stringent regulations. The repercussions of government decisions extend beyond individual investors to impact overall market stability and the evolution of blockchain technologies. Regulatory frameworks are often designed to curb fraud, safeguard investors, and integrate cryptocurrencies into the broader financial system while fostering innovation.

Example:

Consider a scenario where a government introduces rigorous KYC (Know Your Customer) and AML (Anti-Money Laundering) regulations for crypto exchanges. These regulations mandate thorough user identity verification, enhancing security and legitimacy within the crypto space. However, the trade-off is a reduction in anonymity—a characteristic cherished by some cryptocurrency users. Another instance involves a country unveiling plans to launch its digital currency, essentially a digital version of its fiat currency. Such an announcement can significantly impact the demand and utility of existing decentralized cryptocurrencies, as it introduces a new player into the digital currency landscape.

This chapter provided you with a comprehensive understanding of the practical applications of cryptocurrencies in everyday life, such as digital payments and global remittances. It explained how cryptocurrencies like Bitcoin and Ethereum are revolutionizing financial transactions with their secure, decentralized blockchain technology. The chapter also covers the impact of government policies on the crypto market, highlighting the balance between security and anonymity, and the potential influence of national digital currencies. Additionally, it discussed the challenges and future prospects of cryptocurrencies, including volatility, regulation, and the emergence and impact of cryptocurrency Exchange-Traded Funds (ETFs). This comprehensive overview demonstrates the increasing integration of cryptocurrencies into daily commerce and the global financial system.

Chapter 6

Risks and Rewards: Navigating the World of Cryptocurrency Investment

This chapter serves as a comprehensive guide for newcomers to the cryptocurrency market. It delves into the multifaceted nature of cryptocurrency investments, highlighting the potential for significant gains as well as the risks involved. The chapter emphasizes the critical role of informed decision-making, strategic planning, and an understanding of market psychology in navigating the volatile cryptocurrency landscape.

1. Understanding Cryptocurrency

Terminology & Usage: Cryptocurrencies, such as Bitcoin, Ethereum, XRP and Solana, represent a revolutionary form of digital money. They enable transactions that are not only secure due to cryptography but also decentralized, meaning they operate independently of a central authority.

Example: A practical use case is purchasing a movie ticket online using Bitcoin. This transaction is akin to using a mobile payment app, but with the added benefits of security and potential anonymity offered by blockchain technology.

2. Advantages of Cryptocurrency Investment

Volatility and High Returns: Cryptocurrencies are notorious for their rapid and significant price fluctuations. This volatility can be a double-edged sword, offering the potential for substantial returns on investment.

Example: Consider an early investor who purchased Bitcoin when it was merely a novel concept, valued at only a few cents. As the cryptocurrency's popularity and acceptance grew, its value skyrocketed, turning modest investments into fortunes.

Accessibility: The digital nature of cryptocurrencies means that they are accessible to a global audience, requiring nothing more than an internet connection for investment and trading.

Example: This universal accessibility is demonstrated by a scenario where a freelancer in Brazil can receive payment in Ethereum from a client in Australia, bypassing traditional banking hurdles and currency conversion fees.

3. The Pitfalls of Investing in Cryptocurrencies

Market Fluctuations: While the opportunity for high returns is attractive, the same volatility can lead to significant financial losses. Prices can plummet as rapidly as they soar.

Example: The crypto market crash following the 2017 boom serves as a stark reminder. Investors who jumped on the bandwagon at peak prices experienced substantial losses during the subsequent "crypto winter."

Regulatory and Security Risks: The cryptocurrency market is still in a nascent stage regarding regulatory frameworks. This lack of regulation, coupled with the potential for technological glitches and security breaches, presents considerable risks.

Example: The infamous shutting down of FTX exchange and collapse of many CRYPTO Companies where due to security lapses, underscores the importance of cautious investment in secure and reputable platforms.

Technology and Security Risks: Cryptocurrencies rely on complex technology. There's a risk of losing your investments due to technical glitches, hacks, or even losing access to your wallet.

Example: People have lost access to their Bitcoin wallets because they forgot their passwords. There's a famous story of a man who accidentally threw away a hard drive with Bitcoin worth millions.

4. Strategic Planning and Research

Due Diligence: In-depth research into the fundamentals of a cryptocurrency is essential before investing. This includes understanding the technology behind it, the problem it aims to solve, and the team responsible for its development.

Example: Before investing in a promising new cryptocurrency like Cardano, an investor should scrutinize its blockchain technology, the track record of its development team, and its potential for adoption in real-world applications.

Diversification and Investment Horizons: A balanced investment approach, spreading risk across various cryptocurrencies, can mitigate potential losses. Moreover, deciding whether to invest for the short or long term can significantly influence the strategy and expectations.

Example: An investor might choose to allocate a portion of their portfolio to established cryptocurrencies like Bitcoin for long-term growth, while also investing in newer, high-potential altcoins for short-term gains.

5. Buy/Sell Strategies: Dollar-Cost Averaging (DCA)

Dollar-Cost Averaging (DCA)

Stable Investment Strategy: This investment technique involves periodically investing a fixed amount into a cryptocurrency, regardless of its price at the time. This approach can help smooth out the impact of market volatility.

Example: Consistently investing $100 in a less volatile cryptocurrency like Binance Coin every month, regardless of its current market price, can help average out the investment cost and potentially yield more stable returns.

6. Manipulation in Crypto Markets: Understanding the Impact and Strategies

Identifying and Responding to Manipulation:

The cryptocurrency market is often vulnerable to various forms of manipulation, including misinformation, coordinated buying or selling, and the influential actions of prominent figures or groups. These manipulative tactics can artificially inflate or deflate the prices of cryptocurrencies, impacting investors, especially those using leveraged trading.

Impact on Long and Short Positions:

Leveraged trading, where traders borrow funds to enhance their positions, is particularly sensitive to market manipulation. A deliberately created false positive trend can entice investors holding long positions (buying), leading to an artificial price increase. Conversely, market manipulators may trigger rapid sell-offs, impacting investors with short positions (selling), leading to forced liquidation and significant financial loss.

Relatable Examples:

Avoiding Panic Selling: For instance, if a cryptocurrency's price drops suddenly and without clear reason, it might be a manipulation tactic. Savvy investors might recognize this and hold onto their investment or even buy more at the lower price, anticipating a correction once the manipulation is exposed.

Impact of False Information: In another scenario, a group might spread false positive news about a cryptocurrency, attracting more buyers and driving up the price. Once the truth comes to light, the price could plummet, leading to substantial losses, particularly for those who bought at the inflated price.

Counterstrategies:

- **Research and Vigilance:** Investors should conduct thorough research and stay informed about market trends and news to distinguish between genuine market movements and manipulative tactics.
- **Risk Management:** Implementing risk management strategies, such as setting stop-loss orders, can help mitigate potential losses caused by market manipulation.
- **Emotional Resilience:** Developing emotional resilience and

a disciplined approach to investing can prevent impulsive decisions driven by market rumors or sudden price changes.

By understanding the nuances of market manipulation and its potential impact on both long and short positions, investors can develop strategies to navigate these challenges more effectively. Remaining informed, vigilant, and emotionally resilient are key to safeguarding investments in the volatile and often unpredictable world of cryptocurrency trading.

7. Technical Analysis Tools

Understanding Market Indicators: Technical analysis involves using market data, such as price movements and trading volumes, to forecast future price behavior. Resistance and support levels are critical concepts in this analysis.

Example: If Bitcoin has historically struggled to exceed $60,000 (resistance level) but consistently bounces back when it dips near $45,000 (support level), these price points can inform an investor's decisions on when to buy or sell.

8. Influencer Impact and Market Sentiment

Navigating FOMO: The influence of social media and prominent figures can lead to FOMO, driving impulsive investment decisions. It's crucial for investors to make decisions based on research and analysis rather than following the crowd.

Example: A celebrity endorsing a new cryptocurrency might create a temporary spike in its price. However, savvy investors will look beyond the hype and evaluate the currency's actual potential and fundamentals before investing.

This chapter equips new investors with the knowledge and tools necessary to navigate the complex and rapidly-evolving world of cryptocurrency investment. By emphasizing the importance of strategic planning, due diligence, and a balanced approach to risk, it aims to guide investors towards making informed and prudent decisions in this high-risk, high-reward market.

Chapter 10

The Future of Money: Navigating the Evolving World of Cryptocurrency with Practical Examples

In this chapter, we explore the promising future of cryptocurrencies, highlighting recent projects, applications, and use cases that exemplify the potential and direction of this innovative space.

1. The Evolution of Cryptocurrency with Real-World Examples:

Cryptocurrencies have expanded beyond Bitcoin's initial vision. Ethereum's introduction of smart contracts paved the way for projects like Chainlink, which connects real-world data to smart contracts. Binance Coin (BNB), originally a utility token for exchange fee discounts, has grown into a cornerstone of the Binance Smart Chain, hosting a variety of dApps and financial services.

2. Advanced Blockchain Technology in Action:

Blockchain technology now encompasses complex systems. For instance, Ethereum's transition to Ethereum 2.0, incorporating proof-of-stake, exemplifies advancements in scalability and energy efficiency. Polkadot's cross-chain interoperability represents another significant leap, enabling different blockchains to communicate and share information seamlessly.

3. Enhanced Decentralization and Security Innovations:

Projects like Cardano and Tezos focus on enhanced decentralization and security. Cardano's Ouroboros protocol is a notable example of a more environmentally sustainable and secure proof-of-stake model, while Tezos' self-amending blockchain allows for a more flexible and upgradable system.

4. Smart Contracts and dApps: Broadening Horizons:

The proliferation of decentralized finance (DeFi) platforms, such as Aave and Compound, illustrates the growing impact of smart contracts in finance, allowing users to lend, borrow, and earn interest on cryptocurrency holdings. The rise of NFTs, as seen with platforms like OpenSea, demonstrates the potential of blockchain in certifying the uniqueness and ownership of digital assets.

5. From Historical Milestones to Future Outlook:

Reflecting on milestones like Bitcoin's Lightning Network, which enables faster and cheaper transactions, we can anticipate a future where cryptocurrencies are seamlessly integrated into everyday transactions, reshaping how we interact with money.

6. Diversifying Use Cases with Emerging Projects:

Projects like Filecoin, which offers decentralized data storage, and Golem, which enables decentralized computing power sharing, illustrate the expanding scope of blockchain applications beyond mere financial transactions.

7. Financial Inclusion with Practical Solutions:

Cryptocurrencies like Stellar, designed for cross-border payments with low fees, are making financial services more accessible globally, especially in regions with limited banking infrastructure.

8. Crypto Gaming and Its Impact:

Crypto gaming, a novel fusion of gaming with blockchain, has revolutionized digital asset ownership in games. Through Non-

Fungible Tokens (NFTs), players can genuinely own, trade, and monetize in-game assets in the real world, unlike traditional games. This has led to the play-to-earn model, exemplified by games like Axie Infinity, enabling players to earn real-world value. Additionally, crypto gaming introduces cross-game interoperability, allowing the use of assets across different gaming platforms. This innovation not only enriches gaming experiences but also offers new economic opportunities, making it a significant development in the cryptocurrency domain.

9. Market Maturity and Stability Initiatives:

The introduction of stablecoins like Tether (USDT) and USD Coin (USDC), pegged to stable assets like the US dollar, addresses market volatility, providing a more stable medium for transactions and value storage.

10. Evolving Regulatory Landscape and Compliance:

Countries like Singapore and Switzerland are leading the way in creating a favorable regulatory environment for cryptocurrencies, balancing investor protection with innovation support, indicating a positive trend towards global regulatory alignment.

11. Mainstream Adoption and Corporate Embrace:

Major corporations like PayPal and Square's Cash App enabling cryptocurrency transactions, and Tesla's brief acceptance of Bitcoin payments, signal growing mainstream acceptance. Furthermore, the development of Central Bank Digital Currencies (CBDCs), like China's Digital Yuan, indicates a significant shift towards digital currencies by governments worldwide.

12. The Rise of New Cryptocurrencies and DeFi

New cryptocurrencies are emerging, offering enhanced features like faster transactions and improved scalability. Examples include Solana and Algorand, which promise high-speed and low-cost transactions. DeFi, or Decentralized Finance, is a groundbreaking movement that eliminates traditional financial middlemen, allowing for more direct and efficient financial transactions. Platforms like Uniswap and Aave are reshaping how we lend, borrow, and earn interest on assets, all operated on blockchain technology.

13. Digital Ownership Revolutionized

NFTs represent a unique ownership of digital assets, ranging from art and music to virtual real estate and collectibles. Each NFT is distinct and cannot be replicated, making them valuable for creators and collectors. The NFT market is rapidly expanding, with platforms like OpenSea leading the way. The future of NFTs may extend to digitizing physical assets and integrating with augmented and virtual reality, offering a new dimension to digital ownership and creative expression.

14. Expanding the Blockchain Horizon:

Blockchain's potential extends far beyond cryptocurrencies. In supply chain management, blockchain increases transparency and traceability, with projects like VeChain providing real-time tracking of products. In healthcare, it ensures the security and integrity of medical records. The technology is also making inroads in areas like voting systems, offering a secure and transparent way to conduct elections. The future of blockchain lies in its adaptability across various industries, potentially transforming the way we maintain and access records, manage assets, and verify transactions.

15. Central Bank Digital Currencies: The Future of National Currencies

Central Bank Digital Currencies (CBDCs) are like the digital version of the money in your wallet, but they're issued by the country's central bank. They blend the convenience of digital currencies with the stability of government backing.

Real-World Application: China's Digital Yuan is an example. It's a digital currency you can use just like cash, but it's managed by the government, making it stable and reliable for everyday transactions.

In conclusion, this chapter encapsulates the dynamic evolution and future prospects of the cryptocurrency world. From the rise of new digital currencies and the transformative impact of DeFi, to the unique realm of NFTs and the broad applications of blockchain technology, this chapter provides a comprehensive look into how these innovations are reshaping the financial landscape. It also delves into the emergence of Central Bank Digital Currencies, illustrating a significant shift in the traditional financial paradigm. Overall, this chapter offers a forward-looking perspective on the myriad ways cryptocurrencies and blockchain technology continue to innovate, integrate, and influence our global financial systems and everyday transactions.

Appendix I: Safety, Online Scams, and Best Practices in Crypto Investing

Introduction

This section provides critical guidance on navigating the cryptocurrency world safely and protecting your investments against scams and risks.

Online Safety and Security

- **Securing Your Digital Wallet:** Tips include creating strong, unique passwords and enabling two-factor authentication (2FA) for additional security.
    - **Example:** Using a complex password for your wallet and enabling 2FA on exchange platforms.
- **Recognizing Phishing Attempts:** Learn to identify signs like suspicious emails or messages that mimic legitimate sources, urging you to reveal sensitive information.
    - **Example:** An email that looks like it's from a well-known crypto exchange but has a slightly different email address.
- **Identifying Secure Websites:** Verify the authenticity of cryptocurrency websites and services to avoid falling prey to scams.
    - **Example:** Checking for 'https' in the website URL and researching the site's reputation before transacting.

Protecting Your Investments

- **Avoiding Social Media Scams:** Be wary of schemes prevalent on social platforms, such as fake giveaways or investment schemes.
    - **Example:** A Twitter post claiming a celebrity is giving away cryptocurrency might be a scam.
- **Rug Pulls and Pump-and-Dump Schemes:** Understand and identify these fraudulent practices where prices are artificially inflated, then rapidly crashed.
    - **Example:** A new token gets a lot of hype, sees a price surge, and then crashes after the creators sell off their holdings.
- **Verifying Token Contracts:** Investigate the legitimacy and security of token contracts before investing.
    - **Example:** Reading through a token's whitepaper and checking its smart contract on platforms like Etherscan. Best Practices in Crypto Investing
- **Conducting Research:** Emphasize thorough research, including understanding a project's fundamentals, team, and market potential.
    - **Example:** Analyzing a cryptocurrency's use case, technology, and community support before investing.
- **Diversifying Your Portfolio:** Spread your investments across various cryptocurrencies to mitigate risk.

    - **Example:** Investing in a mix of well-established coins like Bitcoin and Ethereum, along with promising altcoins.

- **Risk Management:** Implement strategies to protect your investments, such as setting stop-loss orders.
    - **Example:** Using a stop-loss order to automatically sell a cryptocurrency if its price falls to a certain level.

Regulatory Compliance and Reporting

- **Understanding Tax Implications:** Overview of how crypto investments are taxed and the importance of keeping detailed records.
    - **Example:** Reporting any capital gains from cryptocurrency trading on your tax returns.

- **Reporting Requirements:** Guidelines on complying with local regulations, including Know Your Customer (KYC) and Anti-Money Laundering (AML) laws.

Resources for Further Learning

- **Recommended Reading and Websites:** Curating a list of trustworthy sources for ongoing education about cryptocurrency investment and security.

Safety Precautions and Day Trading

- **Using VPNs:** Employing VPNs to secure your online trading activities, especially when using public Wi-Fi.

- **Example:** Activating a VPN while accessing your crypto exchange account in a café.

- **Maintaining Anonymity:** Be careful about the personal details you share in online crypto communities or forums.
  - **Example:** Using a pseudonym instead of your real name on crypto discussion platforms.

- **Cautious Approach to Social Media Links:** Verify the authenticity of links on social media, which might lead to phishing sites.

Day Trading and Shorting

- **Risks of Day Trading:** Be aware of the inherent risks in day trading due to market volatility.
  - **Example:** The risk of significant losses from sudden market movements during intra-day trading.

- **Strategies for Day Trading:** Utilize technical analysis and risk management tools.
  - **Example:** Applying chart patterns and technical indicators for better trading decisions.

- **Understanding Shorting in Cryptocurrencies:** Grasping the concept of short selling in crypto markets and its risks.
  - **Example:** Shorting Bitcoin when expecting a price drop, with the risk that the market may move against your prediction.

Caution with Influencers

- **Judicious Following:** Scrutinize the advice of influencers, understanding their potential biases.
    - **Example:** Evaluating the credibility of an influencer who frequently endorses specific cryptocurrencies.
- **Unraveling Biases:** Recognizing that influencers might have vested interests in promoting certain crypto assets.
    - **Example:** An influencer heavily promoting an ICO in which they have invested.

Conclusion

This appendix serves as an invaluable resource for individuals entering the cryptocurrency space. It highlights the importance of understanding safety measures, recognizing scams, and implementing best practices to confidently navigate the complex landscape of digital assets.

Appendix II: Cryptocurrency Strategies and Concepts

This appendix delves into various strategies and concepts essential for anyone involved in cryptocurrency investing, covering risk management, regulatory aspects, wallet types, market analysis, and more.

Risk Management

- **Stop-Loss Orders:** Automated instructions to sell a cryptocurrency when it reaches a set price, mitigating sudden loss risks.
    - **Example:** Setting a stop-loss order for Bitcoin at $40,000 to minimize losses during market downturns.
- **Portfolio Diversification:** Spreading investments across various assets to reduce risks associated with the performance of any single cryptocurrency.
    - **Example:** Balancing your portfolio with Bitcoin, Ethereum, and emerging altcoins like Cardano.

Taxation and Regulations

- **Taxation of Crypto Gains:** Understanding the tax implications of buying, selling, or trading cryptocurrencies, which varies by jurisdiction.
    - **Example:** Reporting Bitcoin trading profits on tax returns in countries where crypto gains are taxable.

- **Regulatory Environment:** Keeping up with evolving regulations regarding anti-money laundering and KYC requirements in the cryptocurrency space.
    - **Example:** Complying with AML policies mandated by FinCEN in the United States.

Wallets and Storage

- **Types of Wallets:** Choosing the right type of wallet—hardware, software, or paper—based on security needs and convenience.
    - **Example:** Using a Ledger Nano S for secure offline storage of significant crypto holdings.
- **Secure Storage Practices:** Implementing safety measures like strong passwords, 2FA, and regular backups for your cryptocurrency wallets.

Initial Coin Offerings (ICOs) and Token Sales

- **Risks and Opportunities:** Evaluating ICOs critically, as they can offer high rewards but also carry significant risks.
    - **Example:** The EOS ICO, which showed both the potential and pitfalls of early-stage crypto investments.

Market Sentiment and Analysis

- **Sentiment Analysis:** Assessing market mood through social media and news, which can impact cryptocurrency prices.

    - **Example:** A surge in positive social media sentiment leading to an increase in a particular cryptocurrency's price.

- **Fundamental and Technical Analysis:** Using these analytical methods to make informed decisions.
    - **Example:** Applying RSI and moving averages to determine potential buy or sell points for a cryptocurrency.

Market Liquidity and Volatility

- **Liquidity Considerations:** Understanding the importance of liquidity in the ease of trading cryptocurrencies without significant price impact.
    - **Example:** Bitcoin's high liquidity compared to lesser-known altcoins.

- **Volatility Management:** Employing strategies like trailing stop-loss orders to manage the inherent volatility in the crypto markets.

Staking and Passive Income

- **Earning Through Staking:** Participating in blockchain network operations through staking, earning rewards in return.
    - **Example:** Staking Tezos (XTZ) for network security and receiving staking rewards.

Decentralized Finance (DeFi)

- **Innovative Financial Services on the Blockchain:** Exploring DeFi platforms for lending, borrowing, and earning interest on cryptocurrencies.
  - **Example:** Utilizing Aave for lending and borrowing crypto assets.

Cryptocurrency News Sources

- **Staying Informed:** Following reliable news outlets and crypto journalists for the latest updates and insights.

Market Psychology and Behavioral Finance

- **Emotional Influence on Trading:** Understanding how emotions like FOMO can drive market movements and impact investment decisions.

Dollar-Cost Averaging (DCA)

- **Mitigating Market Volatility:** Regular investment of fixed amounts into cryptocurrencies, regardless of price, to average out investment costs over time.

Tokenomics

- **Economic System of Cryptocurrencies:** Studying supply, demand, and utility aspects of a cryptocurrency to gauge its potential.

- **Example:** Analyzing Ethereum's Ether for its dual role in transaction fees and store of value.

Market Indicators and Terminologies

- **Key Indicators:** Understanding indicators like RSI, market cap, hash rate, whale activity, and sentiment analysis for informed trading decisions.
  - **Example:** Using the RSI to identify overbought or oversold conditions in cryptocurrency trading

By exploring these concepts and strategies, investors can gain a comprehensive understanding of the intricate world of cryptocurrency and make more informed decisions in their investment journey.

Appendix III: Cryptocurrency Common Terminologies

This appendix provides clear definitions and explanations of commonly used terms in the cryptocurrency world, aiding readers in developing a deeper understanding of the digital currency landscape.

Airdrop

- **Explanation:** The distribution of free tokens or cryptocurrencies to holders of a specific blockchain, often as part of a promotional campaign.

Altcoin

- **Explanation:** Any cryptocurrency other than Bitcoin.

ATH (All-Time High)

- **Explanation:** The highest price level that a cryptocurrency has ever reached in its history.

Bag Holding

- **Explanation:** A strategy where an investor continues to hold a depreciating asset, often with the hope that its value will recover.

Bear Market

- **Explanation:** A market where prices are generally falling, often accompanied by pessimism.

Bull Market

- **Explanation:** A market with rising prices and optimistic sentiment.

DYOR (Do Your Own Research)

- **Explanation:** An acronym advising investors to conduct thorough research and due diligence before making investment decisions.

DApp (Decentralized Application)

- **Explanation:** An application built on blockchain technology that operates in a decentralized manner, typically with no single controlling entity.

DeFi (Decentralized Finance)

- **Explanation:** A blockchain-based form of finance that does not rely on central financial intermediaries and utilizes smart contracts on blockchains, primarily Ethereum.

FOMO (Fear of Missing Out)

- **Explanation:** The anxiety or fear of missing out on potential profits, which may lead to impulsive investment decisions.

FUD (Fear, Uncertainty, Doubt)

- **Explanation:** Negative information or rumors spread to create fear and uncertainty in the cryptocurrency market.

Gas

- **Explanation:** The fee paid for processing transactions on a blockchain network, often in the form of a cryptocurrency like Ethereum's Ether (ETH).

HODL

- **Explanation:** A misspelled version of "hold," indicating a strategy to keep and not sell cryptocurrency.

HODLer

- **Explanation:** A term used to describe someone who maintains a long-term holding strategy for cryptocurrencies, regardless of short-term market fluctuations.

ICO (Initial Coin Offering)

- **Explanation:** A way to raise funds for a new cryptocurrency project by selling tokens to investors.

Market Cap (Market Capitalization)

- **Explanation:** The total value of a cryptocurrency calculated by multiplying its current price by its total supply.

Moon

- **Explanation:** A term used to describe a significant increase in the price of a cryptocurrency, implying that it will reach astronomical heights.

Moonshot

- **Explanation:** An investment or project with the potential for significant returns, often with a higher level of risk.

NFT (Non-Fungible Token)

- **Explanation:** A unique digital asset representing ownership of a specific item or piece of content, using blockchain technology to establish verified and public proof of ownership.

Paper Hands

- **Explanation:** A term used to describe individuals who quickly sell their cryptocurrency holdings in response to price declines.

Pump and Dump

- **Explanation:** A scheme where the price of a cryptocurrency is artificially inflated (pumped) to attract investors, followed by a coordinated sell-off (dump) by those who initiated the pump.

Rekt

- **Explanation:** A slang term used to describe significant financial losses, typically in the context of cryptocurrency investments.

ROI (Return on Investment)

- **Explanation:** The measure of the profitability of an investment, expressed as a percentage that indicates the return relative to the initial investment.

Satoshi

- **Explanation:** The smallest unit of Bitcoin, equal to one hundred millionth of a Bitcoin. Named after Bitcoin's pseudonymous creator, Satoshi Nakamoto.

Satoshi's Vision (SV)

- **Explanation:** A controversial cryptocurrency that emerged as a result of a hard fork from Bitcoin Cash (BCH) in an attempt to follow Satoshi Nakamoto's original vision for Bitcoin.

Shill

- **Explanation:** To promote or advertise a cryptocurrency with the intention of encouraging others to invest, often for personal gain.

Smart Contract

- **Explanation:** Self-executing contracts with the terms directly written into code on a blockchain, automating and enforcing agreements without the need for intermediaries.

Stablecoin

- **Explanation:** A type of cryptocurrency that is pegged to a stable asset, like the US dollar, to minimize price volatility.

TA (Technical Analysis)

- **Explanation:** The practice of analyzing historical price and volume data to make predictions about future price movements in the cryptocurrency market.

Token

- **Explanation:** A digital asset or unit of value issued on a blockchain, often used within a specific project's ecosystem.

Token Sale

- **Explanation:** A broader term encompassing various methods of selling digital tokens, including ICOs and Security Token Offerings (STOs).

Wallet

- **Explanation:** A digital tool that allows users to securely store, send, and receive cryptocurrencies.

Whale Accumulation

- **Explanation:** The process in which a large investor or entity accumulates a significant amount of a specific cryptocurrency, possibly signaling their confidence in its future value.

Whale Alert

- **Explanation:** Notifications or announcements about significant cryptocurrency transactions, often involving large amounts of tokens.

Whale Watching

- **Explanation:** The practice of monitoring the activities of large cryptocurrency holders, often with the intent of understanding their market impact.

YOLO (You Only Live Once)

- **Explanation:** An investment strategy characterized by taking high-risk, speculative positions with the hope of achieving substantial returns.

This comprehensive list of cryptocurrency terminologies provides readers with essential knowledge to navigate the complex world of digital assets effectively.

Author Summary

DocThomaz is not your typical financial guru. We're a collective of experienced investment experts and educators who have ventured into the thrilling world of cryptocurrency. Our journey began like yours – curious, uncertain, and eager to navigate the cryptocurrency landscape.

Through years of exploration and learning, we've harnessed the insights, strategies, and simplified explanations that have made our journey profitable and comprehensible. In *Cryptocurrency 101: Your Simple Path to Bitcoin Proficiency,* we share our knowledge, untainted by bias, with one goal in mind: to empower you.

Our book is your key to unlocking the world of cryptocurrency, demystifying its complex nature, and guiding you through the digital gold rush. No false promises of overnight riches, just genuine advice presented in an accessible and unbiased manner.

So, whether you're a seasoned investor or a complete beginner, join us on this adventure to grasp the true potential of Bitcoin and digital coins. The future of finance is digital, and we're here to help you embrace it. Trust DocThomaz as your reliable companion on this exciting journey.

DocThomaz

Made in the USA
Monee, IL
04 November 2026

67380387R00056